THE BERKSHIRE JACK RUSSELLS

Eileen Chatwin

authorHOUSE®

AuthorHouse™ UK
1663 Liberty Drive
Bloomington, IN 47403 USA
www.authorhouse.co.uk
Phone: 0800.197.4150

Published by AuthorHouse 01/24/2017

ISBN: 978-1-4678-7832-6 (sc)
ISBN: 978-1-4678-7833-3 (e)

CONTENTS

ACKNOWLEDGEMENTS

This book is a true story and takes you through the lives of two 2 Jack Russells called Gabby and Boni. Gabby was born at Scarlett Farm, a Jack Russell Farm in Berkshire that is well known for their breeding of Jack Russells, and Boni was born at home with the Chatwin family in Maidenhead.

They so enriched our family life over the years with their loyalty and totally unconditional love for us all, fussing around you when you were unwell, keeping you company when you were feeling lonely, and being such excellent travelling companions when we travelled abroad. I am sure they found it just as exciting as we all did. We often talk about all the scrapes they got themselves into over the years, fighting with other dogs, getting lost, being unwell with dog flu and picking up ticks from the cornfields where they went for their daily walks. Bath time was the worst they never liked being washed, they used to shake themselves all of the time and you would finish up being just as wet as them. As Grahame the father of this family has now passed away we all felt that the time had come for this to be put down in writing so that others might enjoy reading what a joy a dog's life can be. He absolutely adored these two dogs of ours and would have liked to know that this book had been written about them.

Gabby was born in 1976 and died in June 1992. Boni was born in 1978 and died not long after Gabby in September 1992 of a broken heart. She missed Gabby so much she pined until the day she died. There was no consoling her, she just kept moping around all day looking for her everywhere. Dogs, just like human beings, do like to have someone to share things with everyday. They also missed both the girls, Fiona and Yvette when they had gone away to University, but they always had a great welcome when they came home for the holidays, the dogs never left their sides, and I am absolutely sure that they used to talk to each other about what was going on in the family. I think the best days remembered by us all was when they each had their litters of puppies, seeing them born for all of us, that was the most exciting time as none of us had ever seen animals born before, especially our own pets. I feel certain in my heart and am convinced the dogs would love to know that their lives on earth had meant so much to us all and that we had written a book about them. We really think animals make up a family especially when you have children because they are always their best friend and always on the lookout for them. I sincerely hope that their Master, Grahame my late husband of 44 years, has found them on the other side as they were such a joy to him.

This book is dedicated to them all.

CHAPTER 1

THE BEGINNING

HI MY NAME is Gabby short for Gabrielle and my daughter's name is Boni short for Bonifacio which is the name of a town in Corsica. We are Jack Russells and we are going to tell you about the exciting time we had on this wonderful planet called earth.

One beautiful morning on the 4th September 1976 I opened my eyes to find myself lying in a big kennel along with five other puppies. The floor of the kennel had lots of straw in it to keep us warm. A much larger dog was standing over us licking us clean, "Who are you" I asked wriggling to stand on my feet. "I am your Mum silly". "Haven't you got a name" I ask in a very squeaky voice. "Of course I have silly, my name is Daisy and your Dad's name is Rufus, and he will be coming to see you tomorrow". "We have been waiting a very long time for you all to be born and now he just can't wait to see you" she said.

The next day, just as promised, Rufus did indeed come to see us with Farmer Jack who owned the farm. Mum introduced us to him saying "This is your dad Rufus and this is Farmer Jack". Farmer Jack gently lifted Rufus into the kennel and he then went off leaving us alone with him, and then Rufus started licking us too, just like Mum had. "Hello there my beautiful little babies, I am your Dad and I live on the farm as well" he said. "Are you going to stop with us now as well" I asked him. "Well no, unfortunately I cannot stay in your kennel with you all as much as I would like too, I have to share a kennel with some other Jack Russells who live on the farm, they have puppies here on the farm as well, and, I have a job to do during the day". "What do you do then for your job" I asked. "I catch rabbits for the farmer when he goes walking across his many fields".

"Sometimes he sends me down rabbit warrens to

catch the rabbits and once or twice I have got stuck in the warrens, and then the farmer has to pull me out by my back legs, it's alright though it doesn't hurt much" Rufus said.

It wasn't long before long Farmer Jack arrived back at the kennel and said to Rufus "Say goodbye to your Dad little ones, it's time for him to go to work now". What an exciting life he leads I thought. After this first visit Dad came to see us every day and this was when we were allowed out of the kennel and both he and Mum chased us around all over the farmyard, and I thought this was what it would be like forever. There were of course other puppies running around with their Mum's and Dad's as well. It was while we were out of our kennel that Farmer Jack used to clean our kennel out putting lovely fresh straw in, it really kept you warm at night. I never got to know what the other puppies were called because no-one ever gave them a name.

CHAPTER 2

VISITORS

Dogs don't seem to understand time the way human beings do, and time just seems to fly by to us. Then one morning Mum snuggled up to us all in the kennel and said "Today we have some young people coming to see you , and like I told you before, the time is coming for you all to leave me and go and live somewhere else with a new family of your own." "Oh no" I cried, "We like it here with you and Dad". "Where will we live, will we live on a farm like this or will it be in a house like Farmer Jack's?". I asked. "I really don't know" said my Mum "But it will be nice". "Farmer Jack wouldn't let you go to anyone he didn't like" Mum answered.

Later on that morning Farmer Jack gently took me from our lovely warm kennel and brought me out into the daylight. As I looked up to see where he was taking me I saw that there were two little girls standing next to him and he said "She really is a nice little puppy this one, and very special because she is nearly pure white, and this is unusual for a Jack Russell as they usually have brown or black blazes on their bodies or foreheads".

"Please let us hold her" they begged and Farmer Jack gently passed me to the little girl with red curly hair saying "You hold her first then Fiona". Fiona gently stroked me "Aren't you just the most beautiful puppy in the world, and so cute" she said as she kissed me on the nose and cuddled me. "Here Yvette you hold her she is lovely" she said as she passed me over to her fair haired little sister.

Yvette seemed very nervous when she held me and then much to my horror she dropped me. Luckily it was only onto the grass and she quickly picked me up again, "I'm so sorry little doggy, I didn't mean to drop you", she cried. What a silly girl I thought, luckily for me nothing was broken, I was just a little shaken up. I'm only a puppy I thought to myself she should be more careful.

Farmer Jack was talking to the little girls Mum and Dad saying "It will be about ten weeks before she can leave her mother, will that be alright with you". Dad replied "Yes of course it will, we cannot wait to take her home". It was then that I realized that they wanted to adopt me, taking me away from my Mum and Dad and all my brothers and sisters. Oh I thought, is this going to be my new Mum and Dad just like Mum told me it was going to be like. Are the little girls going to be my new family as well. I just hoped the little girl called Yvette wouldn't drop me again. As they were leaving the little girls looked into the kennel and said "Goodbye little doggy we will see you soon". They seemed very excited when they left in their car and drove away.

CHAPTER 3

LEAVING MY MUM

A FEW WEEKS later, mother started making a great fuss of me one morning and said " Well today's the day when you must venture into the big old world, but I am sure you are going to be fine, say goodbye to your brothers and sisters". I turned to them in the kennel and said "Goodbye and I hope you find a nice home as well". Upon that Farmer Jack's very large hand dipped into the kennel and took me out. Rufus my Dad was with him and he let him give me a lick and told him to say goodbye to me. Then he carried me over to a big green estate car where both the little girls were waiting for me, the ones who had been to see me before, along with their Mum and Dad. Farmer Jack said "Here you are girls, she'll settle down very quickly, and I am sure you are going to love her very much, but if you have any problems just call me, just don't forget her injections they are very important". "We won't" replied the girls. Then he whispered something to the girls Mum and Dad about my tail but I did not really understand what he was talking about, my tail felt alright to me. The little girls wrapped me up in a lovely blanket and put me in the basket in the boot of their car.

The girls and their Mum and Dad all piled into the car, but I felt very nervous and sad as we drove away from the farm leaving my Mum, Dad and brothers and sisters behind. I began to feel sick as the car travelled along the winding roads, what if I stand up I thought. I might feel a little better, but I didn't. The girls kept turning round in the car from the back seat to see if I was alright, "Not long now and we will be home", they said.

CHAPTER 4

MY NEW HOME

SUDDENLY THE CAR came to a halt and the boot swung open and Fiona gently picked me from the basket saying "Come along little Gabby let's get you settled into your new home". Who's Gabby I thought, I wonder if it my name, like Mum was called Daisy and Dad Rufus. We must all have names, I rather like that I thought.

Yvette picked up my lovely new basket and blanket and carried it into the house. Fiona gently put me down on the floor and showed me where my basket was in the kitchen. "Now this is where you are going to sleep" said Fiona, doesn't look too bad I thought as I climbed in and snuggled into my blanket, it's lovely and warm in here. Much better than being in that big kennel with just straw, we didn't have any blankets at the farm in our kennel. I felt tired after my journey in the car so decided to have a little snooze in my lovely new basket.

Suddenly I became aware of Fiona and Yvette leaning over my basket, "Come on", they said "here is some food for you, you must be hungry by now". There were two little bowls, one with water and one with some mixed up cereal with milk in it. After a few sips of water they tried to feed me some of the cereal, I had not had this sort before. It tasted different from the cereal they gave me at the farm. They tried coaxing me, "Come on try it" they said, sticking a plastic spoon in my mouth. I soon showed them I did not need to be fed with a spoon, I had learned how to eat from a bowl from my Mum. Not too bad a taste I thought I expect I will soon get used to it, but I can't really tell them can I, because after all I am just a dog.

I ate my food every day just like they wanted me to, and as I got bigger the girls used to bribe me with little chocolate buttons into doing things right, and on this particular day Fiona stood over me in the kitchen and said "Gabby we do not like you wetting the kitchen floor, we're fed up mopping your wee wee up, so we are going to train you to go outside in the garden, do you understand". It was quite funny to watch her telling me this because she kept wagging her finger at me. So I thought o.k. I will give it a try.

First time Yvette put newspaper on the floor just a little way away from my basket to try and encourage me to go to the toilet on it. Then after a couple of hours Yvette would come back again and tell me it was time to go for a wee wee and put me on the newspaper, and as time went by she gradually moved the newspaper nearer and nearer to the back door each time.

Once I got to the back door both Fiona and Yvette took it in turns to bribe me out of the door into the garden, then when I did that and went for a wee wee in the garden I got more chocolate buttons, and guess what I learned very quickly after that. I also learned to bark to tell them I wanted to go outside for a wee wee, but sometimes I just wanted to go outside to chase the birds that were always in their garden.

Chapter 5

NEW ADVENTURES

For the first few weeks I was only allowed in the garden. I could see there were fields by where we lived when we went out in the car, and kept trying to get out when they stopped so I could go for a run. Fiona realised what I was trying to do and said "Sorry Gabby it's for your own good, you need to have your injection before you can go out to the fields for a run, we know you like running about". Of course I did not know what an injection was then so I did not take much notice, so as far as I was concerned the garden was fine for me to play in for the time being.

A few days later Yvette came and put my new red

lead on saying "Come along Gabby it's time to go to the Vets". What's the Vets I wondered. Dad and Yvette put me into my basket in the boot of the car and off we went. We soon arrived at a building which Yvette told me was the Vets. When we went in we sat very patiently waiting for whatever was to happen next. It wasn't just me there, there was a great big dog a cat and a rabbit in a cage. The big dog told me he was a Labrador and that his master was blind so he really needed him and the cat told us she really did not feel very well and could not eat her food so her master had brought her along to the Vets to see what was wrong with her. When I told them I was having an injection they just smiled.

Well I really didn't have a clue what was going to happen but when my name was called Dad picked me up and we went into a room where I was put on this big shiny stainless steel table. "Come on there's a good girl, it won't hurt" said this man pushing this very large needle into my rear end. Well I can tell you it was rather painful and it made me have a little wee wee on their big shiny table, and I wanted to bite his hand, but Dad was holding my mouth shut. "Thank you very much for doing her injection, will she feel ill at all "said Dad. "Not at all, maybe just a little bit sleepy that's all "he said.

13

Then as though that wasn't enough, a few days later just as I was recovering from this injection, Fiona put my lead on this time and picked me up giving me a cuddle and said "I'm sorry Gabby but we have to go to the farm to have your tail docked". What on earth are they going to do to my lovely tail. Why can't they just leave it alone I thought? It was then I realised what Farmer Jack had been talking about to Mum and Dad on the day they collected me from the farm, I had wondered what that was about.

Well, when we arrived at the farm I could hear all these other dogs barking so thought I was in for a bit of fun. The Farmer took me into his kitchen gently stroking me saying "It won't hurt Gabby, you'll be alright in a minute". Once again I found myself on a big stainless steel table. First he rubbed some cream into my tail and then he took out these very large clippers, like the sort you prune trees with, and cut some of my tail off, well I let out such a loud howl, because it really did hurt. Then he put some bandages on it to stop the blood from running everywhere, I really felt like a wounded soldier.

What next? I thought. Injection in my rear end and now my beautiful tail cut off. I just wanted to go home and get in my basket, Fiona was allowed to wrap me in my blanket and to sit on her lap in the car so she could cuddle me on the way home. "It's alright Gabby you will soon forget the pain I promise you" she said. As I lay in her arms I felt very safe but did wonder what else had they got in store for me.

After a couple of weeks my poor little tail was healed and my new adventure was being taken for a walk round the estate of houses where we lived, every day, sometimes it was Fiona and sometimes it was Yvette, the lesson was always the same. When we got to the kerb to cross the road it was "Sit Gabby, I am going to teach you to cross the road properly and when the road is clear we will cross". Well we did this until I knew what had to be done. Next it was Mum's turn and she said "Now I have to teach you not to pull on the lead Gabby and to walk properly because the girls have said you keep tugging on it, and walking in front of them, you seem to think this is a game".

After a very long walk with Mum I got the idea and stopped tugging on the lead and tripping Mum up by walking in front of her.

Chapter 6

REWARDS

After this the girls took it in turns and I got better at it each day. They kept telling me I would get a really special reward for learning to do this properly. Lo and behold a few days later we all climbed into the car and Fiona said "This is your treat for learning to cross the road and to walk properly, remember I told you there would be a special treat."

This turned out to be Burnham Beeches in Burnham which are the most beautiful woods in the autumn, the leaves on the ground lie so thick they rustled as you ran through them, they nearly covered me so you can guess how deep they were. I was allowed off my lead and ran from one tree to another, secretly hoping that I might see a rabbit, or perhaps a squirrel, but no such luck. The girls chased me all over the woods. This is truly a wonderful place for dogs to run around in, all dogs should be brought here. Mum had brought a picnic so we sat in the special picnic area that had been built in these lovely woods. They had some cups of tea and little sandwiches plus some crisps, they all like them. I had some nice doggy chews and some biscuits.

It was beginning to get dark so we had another walk round in between all these tall trees and this time I did see a rabbit, I chased it but didn't catch it. Don't really know what I would do with it if I did.

Chapter 7

EXPLORING

Every day when I played in their lovely garden I liked to dig around the concrete supports under the two sheds, the concrete was only in the four corners so there was a great big space under the shed. I used to get very muddy paws digging like that but never did find anything but a few worms and snails. The one at the top of the garden was where Dad kept all his garden tools, and in the one at the bottom were all Fiona and Yvette's garden games.

There were bird feeders hanging from the roof of the shed at the top of the garden all year round from which the birds were always feeding, try as I might

I never managed to catch one, they were too fast for me. I used to dig round the apple trees and flowers as well to see what I could find. Then I decided that I would dig a big hole just for me then I could hide my little treasures in it, like my doggy chews, bones and stones. No-one will ever find them I thought, but the sad thing was I couldn't always remember myself where I had buried them and had to start all over again.

Then one day when I was out foraging around in the garden I came across two hedgehogs sleeping under the garden shed. "Go away" they cried "this is our home, we know you live in the house and that is your home because we have seen you in there". "Alright, I am not going to hurt you, but do you live under both sheds" I said, "Yes of course we do, at night we move up to the shed near the house because it is warmer" they replied. "Okay, I was only trying to be friendly" I said to them as they scuttled back under the shed. After that I used to see them when I went outside at night to the toilet but they always put their prickly pines up to warn me to stay away. They weren't very friendly.

Then one morning when they were all going out the door Fiona called out "We won't be long Gabby, just going shopping, just stay out of trouble while we are out". After they had gone I was feeling bored so I decided to chew my lovely wicker basket and then one of Dad's slippers. Then I wandered around the kitchen for a while and found a cable that looked interesting, it was coming from the side of the fridge. After I had been chewing on it for a little while there was a large bang which threw me across the kitchen. I lay on the floor for a little while feeling rather dazed, what on earth was that I thought did somebody shoot me.

I felt a little dazed as I lay there but after a little while I began to feel a little better. I thought well let's investigate a bit more, it was lovely and warm at the back of the fridge so I thought I would go in there and have a snooze on a little shelf that was in there. After a little while I woke up and thought I would go back to my basket, but oh no! I couldn't get out, struggle as I might I couldn't get out. I was beginning to panic now, I hope they come back soon otherwise I am going to be here forever.

Well it was autumn and it gets dark early and it was beginning to get dark now, when are they coming back I worried. Then, much to my relief I heard them arrive home and coming into the house Yvette was calling "Gabby, Gabby, where are you?" and all I could manage was a little whimper. Eventually after much searching around they found the chewed up cable and began to pull the fridge out from against the wall and that is where they found me, stuck on the shelf behind the element of the fridge. By the time they got a screw driver to remove the element from the fridge I was shaking like a leaf and very frightened. After they had removed the element and taken me off the shelf Yvette gave me a very big cuddle and said "I don't think you will be doing that again in a hurry". I knew their Mum was not very pleased with me because I heard her saying to Dad that some of the frozen food in the fridge had started to defrost because the electricity had been off.

That evening because I was a little shaky Fiona sneaked me upstairs with her at bedtime but Yvette came in and caught her. "Oh no you don't, you know we are not supposed to have her upstairs in our bedroom, but I won't tell if you let me have her tomorrow night" she said. I found this quite exciting with them fighting over me. Perhaps I might get some treats while I am upstairs, you never know I thought.

But alas, it was not to be, because before long I was discovered upstairs by their Dad and after that I was only allowed upstairs at homework time, but had to come down at bedtime as I was told that it was not healthy for me to sleep on their beds all the time. So during the evening I sat in the front room with Mum and Dad and at bedtime I kept guard over the whole house while they all slept. I did feel very important.

CHAPTER 8

FAMILY HOLIDAY

L ATE ONE NIGHT they started packing up the car, which seemed a little strange to me, but then Fiona came and whispered in my ear, "We are going to the seaside for two weeks holiday tomorrow and you are coming with us so you just be a good girl and go to sleep now and I'll see you in the morning".

I didn't sleep much that night because I was so excited, the seaside, well I had never been before, so to me it was yet another adventure. The next morning we set off for the seaside and soon arrived at the little house they had rented on the seafront. This is Ilfracombe in Devon in Cornwall the girls told me and they took me down onto the beach to show me the sand and the sea for the very first time as I had never seen it before. They took their shoes and socks off and we all went for a paddle in the sea, it was very cold and I found that the sand was sticking in between my nails on my paws. After a while we went back to the house to get dried off and to choose where we were going to sleep now that their Mum and Dad had unpacked the car. While they were doing this I had spied a nice comfy chair that I thought would be good for me to snooze in at night when they were asleep. They had brought my basket but I thought the chair would be much more comfy.

Every day started early and after breakfast we all went down onto the beach and into the sea for a paddle. When we had had enough of that they built sandcastles with moats around them, "Look Gabby this is a castle with moats round it to protect the people living there" Fiona said even though I did not really understand, and every time I got excited I kept knocking them down but they just laughed at me. I really like this seaside I thought. Sometimes we had a picnic on the beach but we kept getting sand in our food, so as we were not far from the house we went back there for our lunch. In the afternoon's we used to go and visit other local towns which we had not been to before. One of them had a little roundabout on the edge of the beach that the girls could ride on, and one had donkeys that you could go for a ride on. Dad used to put me on a lead then to stop me worrying the donkeys.

After a few days my paws were feeling a little sore as the sand was getting stuck in between my nails. Fiona knew they were sore because I kept licking them and she decided then that she would wash my feet and scrub my nails with a little nail brush every night when we came in from the beach.

It seemed like a very long time that we were on this holiday, but then one sunny morning Mum announced to the girls that it was time for us to go home. Oh joy, I thought, no more sand. I felt very pleased at the thought of going back to my nice warm kitchen and my own special garden with no sand.

It did not take long to pack up the car as everyone helped and soon we were homeward bound, hooray I thought.

Chapter 9

VISIT TO SCARLETT FARM

A FEW WEEKS after our holiday when things had got back to normal Mum packed sandwiches and drinks and told us that we going out for the day, me as well. "Come along Gabby you're going to have a lovely day" their Mum said. Where are we going I wondered, what was this all about, they were making a great fuss of me. Well, before long we were driving through the farm gates where I had been born. Panic ran through me, they're not giving me back I thought with horror. They wouldn't do that to me, they love me. I could hear all these dogs barking and looking through the window of the car I could see all these Jack Russells in a field, and I could see my Dad Rufus but where was Daisy I wondered, you never forget what your Mum and Dad look like.

Farmer Jack came over to the car, "Just look at you, haven't you grown into a lovely little dog, got a lovely mate for you to play with today" he said "you should have some lovely little pups, what's he talking about I thought I am not having pups, then he said " Butch is a short haired Jack Russell so your pups will have shorter legs than you, but that will be fine". What on earth is going on here I thought as he led me to the kennel where Butch was lying down. Farmer Jack put me inside saying "Have fun you two". Well we soon made friends and after a lot of chasing each other around began enjoying ourselves. Butch said "What fun this is, do you think they will bring you again" "I don't know but I hope so" I said. Butch gave me plenty of nice licks on the face while we played but it was soon time to say our goodbyes when Farmer Jack came to take me out of the kennel. Mum and the girls were there waiting for me and I could hear Farmer Jack telling their Mum that it had been a successful meeting and that I should have puppies soon. Me have puppies I thought, I am only a puppy myself.

After a couple of weeks after visiting the farm I

began to feel a little sick in the morning and noticed that I had a fat tummy which seemed to be getting bigger each day. Fiona told me I was having puppies soon and that we would all be looking after them Then one night I heard Dad say to the girls " I promise that if Gabby starts to have her puppies in the middle of the night we will come and wake you up". Panic set in then, what will I do I thought, well at around midnight on November 4th 1978 mother nature took over and I delivered all these little puppies, and they were just like I used to be. I couldn't believe it, all mine, this is wonderful. Mum, Dad and the girls were all looking on and Fiona was squealing with delight, "Aren't they beautiful" she said "But look Dad one of the puppies eyes are shut and I don't think she is breathing." Dad quickly picked her up and wrapped her in a nice cuddly towel and massaged her heart.

Then he blew very gently into her mouth to clear her airways and after a little while she opened her eyes and began to breathe again. Dad then put her back in the basket with me and Yvette and Fiona tucked us all up for the night and then they all went off to bed. Is this what being a Mum is all about I thought, and then I knew this is how my Mum must have felt when she had me and all my other brothers and sisters. We had all been born on 17th September 1978 and I know this because I heard Dad telling Mum.

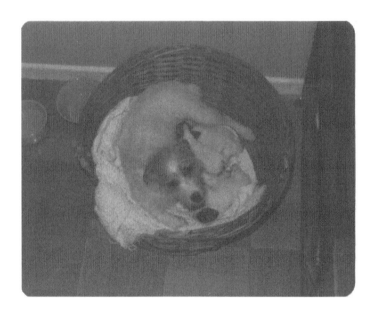

My New Puppies

CHAPTER 10

MY NEW PUPPIES

THE NEXT MORNING it was frantic in the kitchen, Fiona and Yvette wanted to see the puppies again but they were busy having some milk off me. It was their breakfast time as well but they were so excited by all the night's events they told Mum and Dad that they couldn't wait to get to school to tell all their friends about their new puppies, and that they had seen them born during the night.

Within a matter of days all the puppies were scampering all over the kitchen, skidding on the wet floor because they kept wetting themselves with excitement, and they seemed to be permanently hungry as they kept scampering back to me for some more milk. "Stop being so greedy you lot" I told them as I was feeling a little tired now, as they didn't let me have a lot of sleep at all.

Fiona and Yvette had chosen names for them too as they didn't know who was who. They were called Boni, Libby, Spot and Pete. All of my babies were nearly pure white with little blazes on their foreheads, except for Spot who had a large spot on his leg. I was so proud of them all "Just do as I tell you and everything will be alright" I said. Because I also remembered that they would soon be adopted like I was and that they were not going to be with me forever. Better make the most of them while I can, I thought.

Of course over the next few weeks we had lots of boys and girls from their school, Cox Green Comprehensive in Berkshire, visiting us. They all asked me if they could hold my puppies as they had never seen new born puppies before. I told my puppies not to worry as they would not hurt them. "Aren't they lovely" they all cried when they were holding them. As it was the summer they came to visit every week. Yvette kept putting my puppies in her jacket pocket, she said it was to keep them warm. I must admit they all seemed to like it when she did that.

Chapter 11

PUPPIES LEAVING HOME

Alas a few weeks later the girls told me Gail and Richard, their cousins from Birmingham, along with their Mum and Dad, were coming to visit to choose one of my puppies. A few days later they all arrived, Gail was first into the kitchen to see us all. "Oh Dad just look at them they are lovely, can't we have two" asked Gail. "I told you before we came you can only have one" replied Robert their Dad.

They took a long time deciding which puppy they wanted but eventually ended up choosing Libby. "Don't worry Libby they will look after you " I told her that night when she was cuddled up next to me. The next day, just like it was for me, she was wrapped up in a new blanket and put into the back of their car in a nice new basket. Gail and Richard were making such a fuss of her I just knew she was going to be happy. I felt very sad as they drove away.

A few days later the local butcher called Brian came along and chose Spot, they seemed to like each other straight away, and I just knew he would look after him. He was surely going to get enough bones to chew on with a butcher as his master.

After that there was a nice lady called Pamela who wanted a puppy for her children and she chose Pete. He was a very gentle little puppy and just what she wanted for her children. He seemed happy when he went off with her but I was beginning to get a little worried as all my puppies seemed to be disappearing fast. What was going to happen to Boni? She was the only one left now and she nearly died, my last little girl. Surely they were not going to let her go? But much to my relief that night after Pete had gone they told me that Boni was staying with me forever and ever. That night there was just me and Boni in the big basket they had bought for us all but we just cuddled up together and we were fine.

Early the next morning Fiona came to my basket

"Good Morning Gabby, you remember this is your job now, you must show Boni where she should be going to the toilet outside and not in the kitchen." She then whispered in Boni's ear and said " If you don't go to the toilet outside you won't get any treats". Boni like me learned very fast.

Then as a special treat they bought us a lovely new wicker basket each, but they were so good to chew on you couldn't resist it, and they were in tatters in no time at all, after that they were replaced with none chewable baskets which were indestructible, but you could still chew them a little bit.

CHAPTER 12

ARISTOTLE AND TOBY

IT WAS EARLY in the morning and there was something going on with the two girls. "Were having some tortoises delivered today Boni and Gabby, but before they come we have to build a run for them in the garden with some wood and wire netting. This is to keep them safe from you two , we know what you are like chasing little animals.

Their Dad did most of the work in building the run of course, but they did help. Boni and I just wandered around the garden waiting to see what was going to happen next. It was not long before it was finished and we all went inside the house to wait for them. It was not long before we heard a knocking at the back door and when Dad opened the door there stood this man with two tiny little tortoises in a cage. There was great excitement when they saw them and the man spent a little time telling them how they should be looked after, and what to feed them. After he had finished they took him into the garden to show him the run they had made for them. He said " That's a very good run most people do not bother with building them a home of their own and they keep getting lost, sometimes they go into other people's gardens and they never see them again". We just stood looking at them through the wire netting, "Have you come to stay for a long time" asked Gabby. "Well we hope so we like being together" the one tortoise replied. "Well that is like me and Boni, we like being together" Gabby said. Fiona and Yvette brought them some lettuce and chopped up tomatoes for them to eat and they soon tucked into them. "This food looks good and I like this home they have built for us don't you" said the one tortoise to the other.

Yvette turned to Fiona and said "Well are we going to call them the names we decided on, Aristotle and Toby". "Oh I think so don't you" she said. Yvette got a little bowl with some water in and christened them giving them their new names, Aristotle and Toby.

"What was that all about Aristotle" asked Toby. "I am not really sure " said Aristotle "but I am alright are you". I think those are our names.

After this very special day Boni and I used to watch them walking up and down all day long, eating their lettuce and tomatoes. "What's it like being a tortoise" I asked them," you seem to sleep a lot". "Well we like to have cat naps and we get nice and warm when we tuck our heads in" replied Aristotle . "Tell me though, that dog that lives next door, why does he keep barking at us" asked Aristotle. "Well he's not as brainy as us, he's a Beagle you know, they bark at everything, but he cannot hurt you and I think he is afraid of you anyway" said Gabby. So it became the routine for us to go and sit by them in their run and talk to them every day.

Chapter 13

DO I TELL BONI?

Yvette came down this morning picked up Boni and whispered in her ear. She then turned to me and said "Sorry Gabby but its Boni's turn to have her injection, you remember the big needle". "What's the injection asked Boni, does it hurt Mum?". "Well a little bit, but you will be alright" said Gabby. It was not long before Boni was taken off for her injection and I knew what that was like and felt very sorry for her. When Boni came back she couldn't wait to tell me how awful it was and that she had wet the table. "Why didn't you tell me how much it hurt" said Boni. "Well I didn't want to frighten you" I said.

Things were going along nicely, and of course Boni had to have some dog training just like I had so there were lots of walks, but she learned very quickly as I kept telling her when she went wrong.

We talked to the tortoises every day and when we had been out somewhere we used to tell them where we had been, because they don't get out very much, they only see the back garden, sometimes the hedgehogs used to come out from under the shed to listen. The tortoises had never seen hedgehogs before so they were very surprised to see them. Life could not have been more wonderful for all of us.

Then it happened again, just like it happened to me, Boni went off to the farm to have her tail docked. She was very upset when she came home. "Why didn't you tell me what that was going to be like" she cried, "just look at my tail, it's all bandaged up". "It will get better, honestly Boni I promise, you just go for a sleep now and you will feel better when you wake up" I said.

Sure enough after a few days Yvette's Mum took the bandage off and it looked as good as new.

Boni's New Puppies

Chapter 14

BONI'S NEW PUPPIES

ONE MORNING, NOT long after the tail trauma, they told us it was time to visit the Stud Farm again, they told us it was time for Boni to make a new friend. I was glad it was not me, I was too old to be a mum again, and Boni did not realise what they were talking about so I decided to let her find out for herself.

I must admit Boni looked quite pleased with herself when all we went to pick her up. Farmer Jack brought her over to the car when we arrived and started patting my head, "What a lovely girl you have grown into and your daughter is beautiful too" he said. "Mum and Dad I do believe that was a successful meeting and she will be having her litter in a few weeks time" Farmer Jack said. Then we drove off home again. Boni told me later that he had told her that her new playmates name was Rover, and that she had a lovely time.

Not long after our visit to the farm Boni started to get a swollen tummy just the same as I did when I had my puppies. Well I thought is she going to have puppies like I did, I suppose that means I'm going to be a Grandma.

Fiona and Yvette made a great fuss of her during her pregnancy and after a few weeks the day arrived when she was due to have her puppies and sure enough late that night she went into labour and delivered a new litter of puppies.

Of course Fiona and Yvette had demanded to be woke up again when the puppies were being born, and Mum and Dad did, and they all saw all the puppies being born and it truly felt like a miracle. "The date that they were born was 17th September 1979 " said Fiona "and that's their birthdays". All the puppies started fussing round Boni looking for some milk, just like my puppies had done when they were born.

I felt so proud of her doing just what a mum should do, she was very protective and would not let anyone go near them, but after a while she settled down for the night with all her babies around her and went off to sleep.

Once again we had all the girls and boys round from the school to see the new puppies because not many families allow their dogs to have puppies Fiona told me.

After a few days Boni let me make a fuss of her babies and was quite happy to let me play with them. A few days later she let Fiona and Yvette pick up her puppies too. It was a very hot summer so Dad turned one of the sheds into a big kennel for Boni to go in so that the puppies could run around whenever they liked.

They called the two boys Buster and Jack, and the little girls Jill and Lucy. It was not long before they were answering to their names just as my puppies had done.

Ten weeks soon went by and I explained to Boni that the time was soon coming for them to leave home just the way my puppies had. She was very sad and I told her that I would be here for her, I was not going away. Fiona's Grandma Kate came to stay and decided she would like to take Buster home with her. I told Boni that was great news that she would get to see him again when we went up to see her in Birmingham.

When the time came for the puppies to leave home Grandma took Buster with her. Then another lady called Michelle came to see the puppies with her little boy and girl and they took Jack and Jill home with them. "Don't forget their injections" Eileen said when they were leaving, and their tails". I assured Boni that they had gone to very nice homes and she must not worry, but Boni was very sad for a long time and kept coming to me for a cuddle.

We had just got used to Lucy being around when a very nice man called Harry came along and wanted to adopt her so then there were none, I knew she must feel lonely because I remembered what it was like when my puppies left me and I still had her, but she didn't have anyone except me left now.

CHAPTER 15

WINDSOR GREAT PARK

EDDIE AND MARGARET, some friends of Fiona and Yvette's Mum and Dad had come to visit for a few days and were staying at the house and had decided that we should go somewhere special to celebrate Boni's tail being better. Fiona agreed and turned to us and said "Now girls you are going to like this, we are going to a great place called Windsor Great Park where you will be able to run around to your hearts content". I had been before and it was great fun. It had a great lake with lots of ducks and swans, plus lots of large trees and gardens that we could run around. It even had a large Totem Pole at the end of the long walk to run around which all the dog's seemed to like.

Upon our arrival it was not long before Boni soon spotted the animals on the lake, of course she did not know what ducks or swans were but in no time at all she had taken off towards the lake diving in head first. At first she floundered around in the water, she didn't know how to swim, what was she going to do I asked myself, but being a dog she quickly learned how, and off she swam towards the ducks trying in vain to catch them. The ducks and swans either swam quickly away or flew off in all directions squawking their heads off in fright. I ran as fast as my little legs would carry me to the edge of the lake, barking at her to come back, "Boni come back here at once, you will get pecked by one of the swans or ducks, stop chasing them, and have you seen how dirty you are".

The girls were calling out frantically "Boni come back, come on there's a good girl" but she was having such a wonderful time in the lake she took no notice. Eventually as she began to tire of swimming, after all it was the first time in her life she had attempted this, she decided enough was enough and came out. As she crawled out of the lake we could see she was covered in green slime, and by this time rather a large crowd had gathered to look at this cheeky little dog who had dared to swim in the lake and chase the ducks and swans.

They all started clapping their hands when she staggered to her feet at the edge of the lake. She was filthy, Dad said "Well we shall just have to go home, she is filthy, just look at her, and she is shivering too, we cannot leave her looking like this, and if we don't she will probably catch a terrible cold." She was quickly wrapped up in an old towel and put in the boot of the estate car. "What do you think you were doing" I said to her "you could have drowned". She just lay in the towel looking very sorry for herself.

Upon arriving home she was immediately given a cold hose down with the garden hose to get the green slime off her. Luckily for her she was then given a warmer shower indoors. She was lovely and clean when she came out and I said to her "Serves you right my girl, you spoilt the whole day for everyone". Looking very shame faced she came and snuggled up close to me in my basket. "Can I stay with you tonight Mum" she asked "I don't feel very well". "O K " I said.

CHAPTER 16

LOST IN THE FIELDS

THE NEXT DAY I noticed that the back door had not been shut properly so I thought I would take Boni off on a little adventure of our own so we sneaked out the door. It felt very exciting on our own, we even stopped at the kerb to make sure there were no cars coming. Having crossed the road safely we went into the cornfields and today there seemed to be a lot of rabbits around so we started chasing them. Never caught one though, don't think we got enough practice that was the problem. As we ventured further into the cornfields we began to see lots of little field mice running around and it was then that we realised we were lost. We wandered around for ages in amongst all the straw bales trying to find our way back but couldn't. As we lay down for a rest Boni asked "What are we going to do Mum I am thirsty and hungry?". " I don't know " I replied, "I don't know the answer to everything". "Do you think they will come and find us" she asked again.

It was starting to get dark now and I was getting a little worried when I suddenly heard voices calling us. We are saved at last I thought, they have come to find us. "Oh you two are in big trouble" shouted Fiona, "what do you think you were doing going off on your own like that, we thought someone had stolen you, no treats for you two tonight". I really didn't care about the treats I was just glad to be going home. Of course when we got home we were really given a big telling off by Mum and Dad.

Visit to the New Forest

CHAPTER 17

THE NEW FOREST

A FEW WEEKS later Fiona told us we were off on holiday to the New Forest in Hampshire where we were going to meet Uncle Robert, Auntie Diane, Richard, Gail and Grandma Terry and best of all Libby, one of my puppies was going to be there. "Boni you are going to see your sister again, you remember Libby don't you" I said. " How exciting" she cried wagging her little tail. "We will be camping of course in a tent and you can sleep in there with us to protect us from the animals that roam around in the middle of the night" said Fiona. "What animals are they Mum" asked Boni. "Not quite sure, they cannot be that big though, don't worry I will protect us all" said Gabby.

The next day we sat watching while they began packing up the car with a tent, four sleeping bags and their lilo's of course, and there was a big ground sheet that went with the tent and some large poles. There was also two big holdalls "I just hope you have put all the things in there that you need, enough knickers for a week and warm jumpers and trousers, because it can get a little bit cold during the night, it's a good job we have an estate car otherwise I don't think it would all have fitted in the car" said their Mum. They did not put our baskets in and I did wonder where we were going to sleep.

Fiona, Yvette and their Mum were busy filling up a box with food to take on holiday with us and I saw them putting in some tins of dog food. I knew they would not forget us. That was then taken outside and put in the car and Dad said "That's it now the car is full, no more bags , and if you do have any you will have to sit with it on your lap". He shut the boot of the car and came into the warm house.

Next morning we all got in the car and that's when Fiona put our dog blankets in the car out of our baskets and we were allowed to sit on the back seat with them. Boni said "This is lovely isn't it Mum we should do this all the time, it's very cosy". Dad was still outside locking up the house and making it secure. He eventually climbed in the car and off we went on our new adventure.

It is quite a long way to the New Forest so on the way we stopped for a picnic in a nice roadside picnic area. They all had their sandwiches and we had some dog biscuits and some chopped up carrot, we liked these as a snack. We only stayed a little while and we were off again. After about an hour or so we came to these signs that said Brockenhurst and we turned off the main road. I only know that because Yvette was reading the road signs as we drove along.

Soon we came to this large clearing where there were lots of pitched tents and caravans and then Uncle Robert came running up to our car to show us where we had to park. When we got there Uncle Robert had this very large caravan with a big tent attached to it. As we all climbed out of the car Gail came running towards us with Libby in her arms, and Richard was not far behind her. When Gail put her down Boni and I could not stop nuzzling her nose and licking her, we were so excited at seeing her again. She had grown and was now as big as Boni, they were chasing each other round in circles.

"Come on now all of you time to get this tent up" said Dad and they all began to help in putting the tent up. It was soon up and it looked very magnificent. They unloaded all the things out of the car and began putting them in their place inside the tent, and right by the inside flap, which was the door really, was where they put our dog rugs and told us that was where we were going to sleep at night keeping guard.

When this was all over Uncle Robert and Fiona's Dad lit a barbecue and it was not long before we were all tucking into beef burgers, sausages and baked potatoes. Boni and I quite liked sausages.

For pudding they all had some baked bananas which had been baked in foil on the barbecue and Auntie Diane got some ice cream from her little fridge that she had in her caravan. They gave us some as well, just the ice cream, no bananas we didn't like them. We were so happy, three little dogs sharing all this food with them.

In the evening we were all taken over to the big play area where children were playing and Richard decided he wanted to play football so they all joined in, and they let us go and play with them. Of course every time one of us dogs got the ball we used our noses to push it along, the ball was too big for us to hold it in our mouths and they would come chasing after us. It was great fun and we were promised by Yvette that we could do this again tomorrow.

Bedtime, well this was something new and the girls were soon tucked up in their sleeping bags after they had their hot chocolate. I went and laid down by Fiona and Boni decided she should go lie down by Yvette. The grownups were sitting outside talking and listening to some music and I must have dozed off because the next thing I knew their Mum and Dad were in the tent climbing into their sleeping bags. We were told to go and lie on our blankets by the flap which was now closed down to keep us all warm inside. It was a very uneventful night and morning seemed to come quite quickly.

Out came the camping stove the next morning to cook breakfast on and they soon had bacon and eggs sizzling away. Everyone was very excited and soon got dressed because it was a little bit nippy out here in this big field. Soon Libby came over to our tent to see what was going on and before long Dad came over to us and said "Now just here you three we are going for a long walk in the New

Forest, you will have to have your leads on because there are stags and other animals in the forest and you are not allowed to hurt them, but you will see lots of things you haven't seen before, much more interesting than our woods at home".

Everyone got togged up for a nice long walk in the forest and it was not long before suddenly we came upon some stags running through the forest, we all stood still so as not to frighten them, they were so big and I had never seen one before so did not know what to expect. Dad said "Just look at the size of those antlers, I never knew they were that large". Well I know some animals have antlers or horns because Fiona had shown me pictures in her animal books, so I now know what they really look like. As we walked on through the forest we saw lots of rabbits, hares, foxes and very large hedgehogs, much bigger than I had ever seen before. "Mum how much longer are we going to be my legs are tired" piped up Boni, "Mine too" said Libby. " Well, see those tall trees over there, I think we must be on the way back, because I remember passing those trees when we started off on our walk" I answered. Sure enough we were soon entering the large field where our tent was pitched and they let us off our leads.

We went completely mad, chasing each other round and round in circles. There were lots of cow pats and we kept rolling in them and by the time we had finished we were very smelly so they put us under the hose pipe for a shower, it was very cold the water. Won't be doing that again in a hurry I thought.

Then it was tea time again, barbecue was lit with lots of nibbles for the grownups and girls while the food was cooking, and we were given our dog food followed by some special chocolate treats before we all went to sleep for the night. I really do not know what grownups find to talk about all night.

We had several days of beautiful sunshine and then the rain came down, and did it pour. The Mum's and Dad's wondered if we should pack up and go home but it was decided to give it another day to see if it stopped. Well the next morning our tent was filled with water and the Lilo's that the girls and Mum and Dad were sleeping on were floating in the water. When they got up they all had to put their wellingtons on and it was decided that we should pack up and go home. What a mess, everything was covered in mud, it was going to take ages to get it all cleaned up.

After big hugs and kisses all round with the grownups and the children it was time to say goodbye to little Libby, we licked her nose and I said to her "Don't worry we will see you again". With that everyone climbed into their cars and we all set off home.

CHAPTER 18

GRANDMA AND GRANDDAD

ABOUT A WEEK later Fiona and Yvette sat us down and said to us "Look you are going to stay with Grandma and Granddad in Solihull and we are going to take you there today, it's only for a little while because we have to go away with Daddy to America". "You know they will look after you and we will be back soon I promise, they have a lovely garden for you to play in, and they will take you for walks as well, but you know that you have been before".

Soon afterwards all our belongings including our dog baskets were put into the back of the car and after a long ride we finally arrived. All our toys and blankets, including our baskets were unloaded from the car. Grandma and Granddad made a great fuss of us and after lots of cuddles from Fiona, Yvette, Dad and Mum, they drove off and left us behind. "We will be alright Boni, I will look after you" I said. That night when we lay snuggled in our baskets we both knew we were going to be alright.

Every day Grandma and Granddad took us for long walks in the woods where we were allowed to chase rabbits and field mice, never caught any though. Boni was a very naughty dog though, she kept digging up Grandma's flowers and vegetables. She would carry them into the kitchen in her mouth as though she was giving Grandma a present. Grandma used to say to her "thank you very much Boni but I don't think you should dig up any more". Granddad told her off but she didn't take any notice. So, sometimes she didn't get a treat at the end of the day, and after a while she realised what she was doing was wrong and she stopped doing it.

As a special treat Uncle Robert, Gail and Richard brought Libby over to see us and we had a lovely run around in Grandma and Granddad's garden. Libby was so excited at seeing us again so soon. But alas it was soon time for her to go home again. We gave her lots of licks and nuzzles, it was all over so quickly.

Time seemed to pass very quickly and it certainly did not seem like six weeks since they had gone away but early one morning we heard voices shouting "We're back Gabby and Boni, where are you?" "It's us called Fiona and Yvette, we've come back just as we promised". After cuddling us for a while they gave their Grandma and Granddad big hugs, and then there were presents for everyone from America, squeaky toys for us and some nice goodies for Grandma and Granddad, not quite sure what they were but they liked them. Come on called Grandma from the Dining Room dinner is ready and while they all tucked into their roast dinner we ate ours and then played with our new toys.

Soon it was time to go home and Grandma and Granddad kissed us both goodbye and said they would see us again soon. I felt sad when we left because we had enjoyed ourselves while we were there.

CHAPTER 19

FLYING

L IFE SOON GOT back to normal once we were back home again, foraging away in our garden, chasing the birds, and of course seeing Aristotle and Toby again. They had been staying with Fiona's friends and they told us that they had had a wonderful time. Of course this did not last for long because it never did in this house, there was always something going on.

Yvette and Fiona came into the kitchen looking very serious, and I did think to myself oh no!, what now, and then we found out. "Now look here Gabby and Boni we are going away again, but this time you are coming with us, we are going to live in Japan in a place called Tokyo". " It is a big city and they do have parks for you to run about in and we will take you for long walks when you get there" said Yvette . "You will have to fly in a plane though to get there, but you will be in two kennels together on the plane and we will be there to pick you up, so don't be afraid it's going to be alright" said Yvette.

"You two are lucky though, you know Aristotle and Toby have got to go back to the shop because there is no one to look after them for such a long time" said Fiona rather sadly. "Mum" said Boni "what is flying?" "I am not sure, but I think it's going in one of those aeroplanes we see up in the sky" I answered. "Wow" she said "how are we going to get up there". "Not quite sure about that at the moment Boni I will have to think about it " I said.

Packing up soon began again only there were a lot more suitcases this time, five in all plus two large packing cases. There they sat in the hall just waiting to go and then the next day a big van arrived on the drive and took the packing cases away but left the suitcases in the hall.

Then another big van arrived on the drive, we could see through the glass in the front door everything that used to come on our drive, and then there was a knock on the door. Fiona opened it and there stood the driver of the van with two kennels one in each hand. He came into the kitchen to show us the kennels and Fiona asked him why there was newspaper in them. "That is to keep them warm" said the man. After many kisses and cuddles we were gently lifted into our new kennels and loaded into the big truck. "See you soon" called out Yvette and Fiona.

It did not seem very long before we stopped and we guessed we had arrived at the airport. We were unloaded from the van and taken into a large warehouse where there were other animals in cages and dog kennels. There were cats, dogs, birds, snakes, monkeys and other animals, just like the pictures Fiona had shown us in her animal books, and some others which I did not recognise at all. All the animals seemed to be talking at once, "Hello you two are you together, you look the same, I am going to a Zoo" said the tiger. "They don't have dogs in Zoos so where are you going?" said the monkey. "A place called Tokyo to live with our owners in their flat" I answered. But it was very hard to hear what they were saying because it was so noisy. The cats were crying because they were unhappy but the birds kept chirping because they felt happy. They liked to travel they told me.

Then some men arrived and started carrying all the cages and kennels onto the plane. Once on the aeroplane the snake kept hissing at everyone but I thought he was just a bit scared. Then a man appeared and put some food in everybody's kennel or cage. "What's this food" said the big ginger cat to me "tastes like dog food, do you think he got it mixed up". "Well I don't think so, mine tastes alright" I replied. Some of the animals appeared to be asleep, had they given us something to make us sleep I wondered, and of course I soon joined them. Several hours later I woke up because I needed to stretch my legs but there was not a lot of room to turn round and the newspapers that they had lined the boxes with began to shred. I looked over at Boni and I could see that her white fur was slowly turning grey from the ink off the newspapers so I expected mine was too. "Surely we must nearly be there Boni, I'm tired being in this box" I called over to her in her kennel.

"You haven't got a lot or room in there have you mate" said a rather large animal that was lying stretched out in his cage. "No we haven't" said

Gabby "But where are you going to in Japan you cannot possibly be somebody's pet your too big" I said. "I am a leopard silly and I am going to a famous Zoo by Mount Fuji where there are lots of other animals". "In fact most of the animals on this plane are going there, we were talking about it at the airport before you came". "You should come and see us at the Zoo when you have settled in your new home" said the big leopard. The snake who had been hissing so much at the airport was getting quite agitated, "You know our owners are all up there on the top of the plane, I hope they don't forget us when they get off" he said. "I'm not going to a Zoo, I live with a lovely lady called Miranda and we have a nice house to go and live in" he said. "I didn't know snakes lived with people I thought they lived in the Zoo" I said. "Well most of us do live in the Zoo but special snakes like me who have been trained live with people" he said.

The engines on the plane started to get very noisy again so I guessed we would be landing soon. " I think we should all say our goodbyes now because you won't be able to hear yourself think soon with those noisy engines" I shouted to all the other animals.

After we were unloaded from the plane we were put in a room where there were lots of other animals and I could see this large man with a white coat on, who we presumed was the Vet, having been to a Vet before, especially as he had a large hypodermic needle in his hand. He was going round all the animals and giving them injections in their bottoms. "What is he doing" I asked the tiger. "That's your rabies injection, all animals have to have them when they come into foreign countries but you will be alright it doesn't hurt that much." he told us.

Well it was a very noisy night because all the animals were talking about where they were going and about how exciting it was going to be. A new adventure for us all I thought and Boni was obviously enjoying all the excitement too. Monkeys were the ones who did the most talking, they never seemed to stop.

CHAPTER 20

OUR NEW HOME IN TOKYO JAPAN

A FEW DAYS later we were put back into our kennels by two policemen into yet another van. "Where to now?," I asked Boni. After a short journey in the van we stopped, and when they lifted our kennels out we could see we were outside a block of flats. This we were to find out shortly was where our new home in Tokyo was. We were taken up in a lift to an apartment inside the block of flats and much to our delight, when the lift doors opened, eagerly awaiting our arrival were the whole family. We were so overjoyed to see them we could not stop barking with delight.

First we were given a bath as we were nearly black

from the ink off the newspapers and then we were shown where our sleeping baskets had been put. They were in the long corridor that ran right through the apartment, one was outside Fiona's bedroom and the other outside Yvette's bedroom. "We have put your baskets here so you can keep guard at night," said Yvette.

We were very hungry by this time and were soon given a nice bowl of dog food each. "Yum yum this is delicious, I was so hungry weren't you" "I said to Boni. After we had eaten the girls took us off for a walk around the streets of Tokyo to stretch our legs. When we came back they showed us their new bedrooms and told us we could visit them in their rooms just like we had at home. "Whoopee Boni we are home again with our family don't you think this is just great" I said. "Oh yes Mum it's lovely" said Boni. Then we settled down for the night and I know Boni was just as happy as me.

"It's the weekend today and we are not going to school but going to show you where it is, and if you are good then we can have this walk every day" said Yvette. "Mum will come with us of course so she can take you home again, I think you will like that won't you Gabby and Boni" said Fiona.

As we walked the streets on our leads the next day the girls pointed out the small houses that the Japanese lived in and told us that the futons hanging over the rails on the outside of their houses were their beds. Yvette said " They hang them over the rails at the front of the house during the day to freshen them up because they use their bedrooms as a living room during the day and a bedroom at night".

The people here in Tokyo were not very tall and seemed to talk in a funny language that we did not understand, even the family did not understand them all the time. When we were taken out on our leads for a walk the Japanese children used to pat us on our heads and tell us what lovely dogs we were. Well, that's what the girls told us they were saying. Mind you when we went out at night the Japanese dogs kept jumping out from their houses barking like mad at us, but they couldn't reach us because they were chained up and their leads were not very long.

In Japan we found that the all dogs have to be kept on their leads because of rabies. So in the evenings Mum, Dad and the girls took us to a very quiet lane by our apartment where we could have a jolly good run, back and forth from one end of the lane to the other. Fiona told me they would have been in terrible trouble if we had been caught, so we had to do as we were told. Dogs weren't allowed to pooh outside in the streets either, and if you did your owner's had to scoop it up and put it in little doggy bags which you then had to put into the bins that were on lamp posts along all the streets. We always carried some with us when we went out for a walk just in case.

One day we heard this large high pitched screaming noise going on and on. Fiona rushed into the apartment, "Come on Gabby and Boni we have to go to our assembly point at our School because that noise you can hear is warning us about an earthquake" she told us. She put our leads on to go and it stopped. "That's a relief we don't have to go now because it has stopped but if it had carried on we would all have had to go where we would be safe at the School". " Those signs I have showed you in the streets tell us what number it has reached on the Richter scale and if it ever reaches seven we are supposed to evacuate and go to our school for protection, taking our supply of water and food with us". "We have to keep a supply of these goods here at home just in case" she said. "That was a near one I said to Boni, I wonder where we would have slept" I said.

During the day when everybody was out I used to challenge Boni to races up and down the apartment corridor, just to see who could get to the other end first. Of course I always won because I had longer legs than Boni. At night it was a bit creepy though because great big cockroaches came out, they were like big ugly spiders, and they crawled around when everyone was asleep. One night I cornered two in the corridor "Where do you think you are going" I asked them. "Just for a walkabout, what's it to you anyway we live here all the time you don't" the big fat one said. "Don't you hurt anybody or I will kill you" I said. "If you can catch me" the big one said scuttling off down the corridor. After that they used keep out of our way. Sometimes they would come up the plug holes during the night so they would be in the bathrooms when the girls went for their showers in the morning, and boy did they scream if they saw them. They had Mum and Dad running round trying to kill them. That was when we realized they could fly as well. Horrors of all horrors to see them flying.

CHAPTER 21

CHRISTMAS IN TOKYO

URING THE NEXT few days, when we were being taken out for a walk I noticed all these Christmas Trimmings going up in the streets, just like at home. "Look Boni" I said "it must nearly be Christmas and won't that be nice, just look at all those pretty trimmings ".

One day a large parcel arrived and the family got all excited. "I wonder what's in there" I asked Gabby. "Well Fiona told me it was going to be Christmas soon, you remember I told you other day when we were out that I thought it was, you remember we have a Christmas tree with fairy lights and lots of lovely presents stacked underneath it, well it's that time again". I said.

By the time they had the parcel unwrapped, and we helped of course, pulling the brown paper off, we could see there were smaller parcels inside wrapped in Christmas paper. "Look Gabby and Boni presents for you here" Fiona said. But right in the middle of the parcel there was one large pudding basin and Yvette picked it up saying "Look Grandma's sent us one of her home made Christmas Puddings and some suet to make the stuffing for our turkey, isn't she kind". Well of course everyone was delighted with the presents but they were put away until Christmas day.

On Christmas day there was no snow like they had at home but it was a lovely sunny day and they had a lovely Christmas tree with fairy lights and presents all stacked underneath it. Mum and Dad had invited Al and Joanne with their two little girls, Jennifer and Susan, who lived across the road from us in another apartment to Christmas Lunch.

It wasn't long before there was a knocking on the door and Mum and Dad welcomed them in wishing them a Merry Christmas. "Time for a little celebration" said Fiona's Dad. "Would you like a glass of punch". "Yes that would be lovely" they replied. "Eileen we would like you to accept this Pumpkin Pie and Pecan Pie as a little gift from us, this is what we usually have on Thanksgiving Day in America when we celebrate Christmas, I hope you like them" said Joanne. "What a lovely thought" said Eileen, "thank you so much".

When they all sat down for dinner everybody seemed to enjoy Fiona's Mum's roast turkey with the home made stuffing, sprouts, roast parsnips and roast potatoes. This was then followed by Christmas Pudding and Custard the usual pudding had at Christmas in England. After they had all finished Joanne said "Thank you so much that was delicious we have never had turkey before with all those vegetables". Of course we were treated to our Christmas Lunch as well with lots of turkey and dog biscuits and gravy, we like gravy.

Everyone was so full up it was decided that the pies that Joanne had brought were to be eaten with their afternoon tea. When they started pulling the crackers it made us jump, it was such a large bang, but we soon got used to it. They played games which they called pass the parcel when someone got a prize at the end. They even played charade's that seemed to be fun because they got quite excited.

The girls had lots of presents, and of course we had lots of doggy presents too. We just liked being there with everybody.

A little later on in the day they all had either the pumpkin pie or the pecan pie with a little cream. Yvette said "This is delicious, will you learn to make this Mum, it really is yummy". Mum said she would of course. I whispered in Boni's ear "I hope they give us some a bit later". "I'm still full from my dinner" Boni said.

Very soon the guests left and Mum and Dad sat down to talk to the girls about Boxing Day which they told them was the next day. It was decided by Dad in the end that we were all going to go on a coach ride up to Mount Fuji. "Did you hear that Boni, perhaps we might see some of the animals we met at the airport, some of them were going to that Zoo" I said. We caught the coach the next morning and we were told that we had to behave on the coach or they would make us get off. It was quite a long ride on the coach and when we got off we could see the snow on the Mountain and it was very cold. We all made our way to the entrance to the Zoo and once inside I was busy looking to see if I could see the big tiger we met. When we got to the big tigers cage there was more than one in there and I could not see him. However he had spotted us and he let out a big roar of welcome to us, the girl's parents of course did not understand what he was saying but we did. "I never expected to see you two again, but how are you" he asked. "Fine we are really enjoying Japan, what about you I asked". "It's lovely here, the cages are kept nice and clean and the other animals are all nice" he replied. "Come along you two" Dad called out, "what are you dawdling about at". "Come on Mum it's time for us to go" said Boni. There were lots of other animals to see but soon it was time to go home again. "Wasn't that a lovely day Boni and Gabby, did you enjoy yourselves we did" said Fiona.

CHAPTER 22

OUR HOLIDAY

THE SUITCASES CAME out again a few days later so I thought it must be holiday time again for all of us. "Where are we going Mum" Boni asked. "I don't know but it will not be long before they tell us" I said and sure enough Yvette took us to one side and said "Sorry girls were off to Hawaii and you cannot come with us". "Oh no Boni we have to go back to those kennels again, but don't worry I will look after you". I said.

When we arrived at the kennels the next day they put us in a big pen to have a run around with the other dogs so we could have a bit of fun. "Hello you two, nice to see you again" said a big Labrador whom we had met when we arrived in Japan before. "Bet your owners like mine have gone on holiday, they always put us in here" he said. " It's o.k.in here though, they are very nice it's just like being on your own holiday " he said. Wasn't long before some of the dogs starting fighting so they put us back in our kennels for the night. They gave us lovely food every day and we did have great fun playing with all the other dogs. The two weeks went very quickly and it was nice to have other animals to talk to.

When they came back off their holidays they couldn't wait to tell us how beautiful Hawaii was, and that it was a shame we could not of gone with them, but to make up for that it was decided that we would all go on a trip on the Japanese Bullet train.

The next day we were got ready for our trip and off to the Station we went. First we had to go on the local train into Tokyo, that is where we boarded the Bullet train. It did not take long to find some nice seats. "Look girls " Yvette said holding us up to the window, "those fields all have rice growing in them and they are called paddy fields, and the Japanese eat rice with nearly all their meals".

The train took us to a little village where we got off

for a walk round but we only saw the small Japanese people who lived there in their little houses. Soon it was time to go home and we could not believe how fast this train travelled.

CHAPTER 23

OUR JOURNEY HOME

A FTER A FEW weeks the dog kennels were brought out of the cupboard again. " What's happening now "Boni asked me. Yvette and Fiona sat us down once again. "Now look here girls you are going home, but you will have to go into kennels first until we get back as well" said Fiona. "Oh no" said Boni, " not that noisy aeroplane again". "Don't worry" I said, "we might meet some of the animals we met when we came out and that could be nice". That night we had lots of kisses and cuddles and they told us that it would not be too long before we were re-united with them.

It was late afternoon when the van came to collect

us but the man was very kind when he put us in our kennels before taking us down to the van. "Bye Japan" said Boni "Mum and I have enjoyed ourselves". "Come home soon" I said barking at the girls, " we are going to miss you". But of course they did not understand what I was barking at.

Our flight home was very uneventful, didn't see any animals we knew.

When we arrived back home we were taken to some very nice kennels in Binfield where they made a great fuss of us. They had given us a nice bath, as once again we were covered in newsprint off the newspapers, they gave us a very nice meal and showed us the double pen we would be sharing so that we could be together, they told us that they had been told that we were mother and daughter and that we liked to be together.

"Well here we are again Boni, but I will look after you till they come home" I said as we cuddled up for the night. We had not been here before but it was very nice and the people who looked after us were very kind.

Soon our fur grew fast and furious to keep us warm,

it was Winter so we needed our fur to be thick, well it became very thick which gave us nice woolly coats like baby lambs, as we were out in the open a lot of the time. There were lots of other dogs in the kennels so there was plenty of talking going on."How long you in for "asked a Great Dane, "Only a few weeks " I answered rather haughtily. "They all say that, but it's always six months that's the way it is" he said with a laugh. Six months I thought with horror they won't even know who we are when they come back. There were Labradors, Poodles, Corgi's, and lots and lots of dogs, we used to play with them when we had our daily play session. We used to sit there and say well I am a Jack Russell what are you, the poodle thought she was the best dog in the world, but it used to be quite fun finding out what breeds all these other dogs were.

One day we had some visitors who were neighbours from our old house where we used to live. "What are they doing here" I asked Boni, "has something happened to Fiona and Yvette" I said. Of course we did not know the answer to that but we were very excited to see someone we knew. They had brought us some little doggy treats and made a great fuss of us. After that they used to come and see us every week, and they kept telling us that the girls would be here soon to collect us. Spring came and went and we were just beginning to enjoy the Summer after a very long cold winter and wondering when they were ever coming home.

CHAPTER 24

THE FAMILY'S RETURN

Boni and I were just mooning around our dog pen one morning after our run about when we heard these voices calling our names, "Gabby, Boni come here, come here." Fiona and Yvette were standing by the fence outside our kennel waiting for us. Oh my goodness, here they were at last. After a lot of tail wagging from both of us and lots of cuddles we were soon loaded into the car and taken back home where we belonged.

The joy of seeing everyone again and running around sniffing the garden again, it felt wonderful, all our familiar haunts, nothing had changed. Boni was so excited she kept wetting herself.

Never again, I thought don't leave us ever again. The next day we were taken to Linda's, the lady who kept our fur coats trimmed. Well they were so long it took her nearly all day to strip us down. We looked very smart when she had finished us. When Mum came to fetch us she was very impressed with the way we looked and thanked Linda very much for the lovely job she had made of both of us when she paid her. We soon settled back into our normal routine and I kept telling Boni everything was fine now.

CHAPTER 25

NORFOLK BROADS

A FEW WEEKS later we were off again, like I said before there was never a dull moment. This time we all went to the Norfolk Broads and when we arrived we had another little cottage to stay in. I did not know that the Norfolk Broads were all little rivers running from one town to another till we got there. We used to hire a boat for a day and Dad would steer it, sometimes we had locks to go through and they used to tie us up when we went through these in case we jumped in. That would be dangerous Dad told us as we could drown. Sometimes we just used to take a picnic and have long walks along the river banks, sometimes they used to let us go in for a swim, and it was lovely.

One day though Boni and I started fighting in the back of the car, Dad told us to stop but Boni wouldn't. Dad stopped the car and opened the boot and put his hand in between us to try and stop us and he got bitten by accident. There was blood everywhere and that soon stopped us. "You naughty girls, look what you have done, I shall have to find a hospital now to get it bandaged up, what do you think you were doing" Dad said. We both sat in the boot of the car with our heads bowed down, we knew we were in big trouble.

Dad got back in the car and Mum was looking at the map to see where the hospital was and then we set off. Before long we arrived and they went off into the hospital. When Dad came out his hand was all bandaged up, "Just look what you have done" he said," and I have had to have a big injection in my bottom as well, just like you have at the vets".

They gave us some water to drink and bowls with some food in for us to have while they ate their sandwiches before we set off back to the cottage.

The next day they packed up the car and Boni and I realised we were going home. By this time though

Dad had calmed down and he gave us a nice cuddle " Now listen you two I know you didn't mean to bite me but must promise not to do that again" he said.

I'm Gabby

I'm Boni

CHAPTER 26

THE END

AFTER ARRIVING HOME I was rushing upstairs after the girls when I had this dizzy spell and fell all the way down to the bottom. Everyone rushed to see what had happened and after I came round, they told me I had fainted and fell down the stairs. It was then I realised I had wet myself because the carpet underneath me was wet.

This was unusual for me as Boni and I were very well house trained. No-one made a fuss though they just cleaned it up and put me to bed.

That was not to be the end of the incident though, oh no, might have guessed, Yvette was there the next morning "Hi Gabby we are just taking you to the Vets to see what is wrong with you". When we arrived at the Vets we sat and waited our turn and before long my name was called, Dad and Yvette took me in and put me on the big stainless steel table. The Vet gently picked me up saying "come along old girl let's have a look at you and see what is wrong".

He had these things in his ears with long cables on with a silver thing on the end. "This is my stethoscope and I am just going to listen to your heart" he said. He put this on my heart to hear how fast my heart was beating, and told Dad that I must have had a heart attack. But not to worry he would give us some tablets and I would be fine. "She is getting old now and must take things a little easier, don't let her get too excited about things" he said. When I got home I told Boni what had happened and after that she used to fuss round me telling me it would be alright she would look after me.

Boni was true to her word right up until the day I died, this was very sudden and I was very sad to leave them all. The girls cried and Mum and Dad were very sad and after my cremation they had a little ceremony and my ashes were buried in the back garden under a new blossom tree which they planted and named after me.

After I had died I watched a very sad Boni grieving, she was not used to being on her own. For nearly a whole year she wandered around in the garden like a lost soul. Mum and Dad took her on trips to the Norfolk Broads where we had all been on holiday but nothing seemed to get her excited any more. The whole family used to fuss round her but she was unhappy. When she died she was cremated too and put alongside me in the garden under another blossom tree. There was a lot of sadness in the family home where we had lived and we realized how much they had loved us over the years, and of course how much we had loved them.

When Boni and I met up again in heaven we soon realized what a wonderful life and exciting time we had had with Fiona, Yvette and their Mum and Dad. Not too many dogs get treated this well, travelling half way across the world and back again and to have such a wonderful and exciting time as well. I think this is what you called living a dog's life.

Goodbye from Gabby and Boni.